Famous Entrepreneurs

Legends and Game Changers

By Rachel Grack

Eureka!

Eureka! books turn real stories into unforgettable experiences. This nonfiction imprint sparks curiosity, encourages critical thinking, and engages middle-grade readers. *Eureka!* books empower young minds to explore the stories of the real world, one fascinating fact at a time. Unravel the power of knowledge and lifelong learning with *Eureka!*

This edition first published in 2026 by Bellwether Media, Inc.

Library of Congress Cataloging-in-Publication Data

LC record for Famous Entrepreneurs available at: https://lccn.loc.gov/2025024354

Editor: Betsy Rathburn Series Designer: Jeffrey Kollock Book Designer: Josh Brink

Printed in the United States of America, North Mankato, MN.

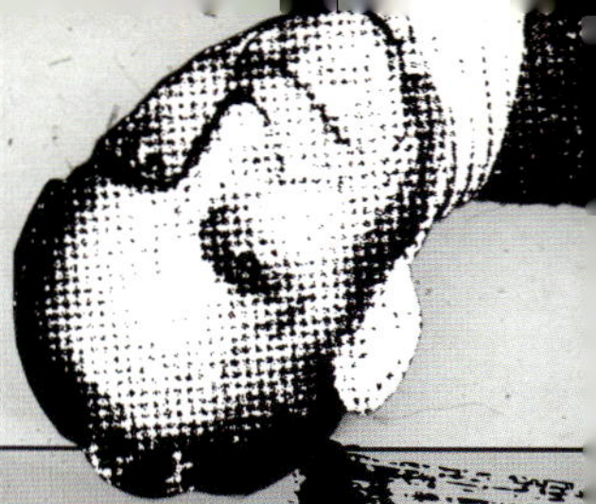

TABLE OF CONTENTS

ENTREPRENEURSHIP HISTORY

Starting a new business can be risky and expensive. Entrepreneurs are willing to take financial risks for potential **profit**. But many are motivated by more than money. They hope to make a positive impact on the world. They create new products or services to solve problems.

Building any business requires **capital**. Funding is one of the biggest obstacles entrepreneurs face. Some choose to build their company through personal savings, loans, and initial sales. Others raise **seed money** through partners or investors. **Crowdfunding** is a common way for small **startups** to go into business.

The first entrepreneurs were traders and merchants. People **bartered** one good for another. Trade routes developed. One of the most famous was the Silk Road. This network of trade routes covered around 4,000 miles (6,437 kilometers) between Asia and Europe. Traders traveled it from 130 BCE to 1453 CE. They transported silk, glassware, porcelain, tea, and spices.

Starting in the 1700s, the **Industrial Revolution** brought machinery and factories. Mass production led to wealthy companies and industry **tycoons**. Today, entrepreneurship is a booming trend worldwide. Many businesses are run entirely online.

TIMELINE

AROUND 7500 BCE
long-distance trade of obsidian begins

STARTING IN 130 BCE
traders transport goods between Asia and Europe using the Silk Road

PAINTING OF FACTORIES DURING THE INDUSTRIAL REVOLUTION

1700s CE
the Industrial Revolution makes it faster to manufacture products

1800s
the invention of the internal combustion engine leads to greater advances in technology and business

EARLY 1900s
the rise of cars and airplanes leads to changes in business practices

1970s
groundbreaking hardware and software increase home computer sales

1990s
the rise of the internet leads to many new online businesses

2016
TikTok is founded, allowing businesses to reach a large audience of young people

2020
the COVID-19 pandemic pushes consumers to shop online, resulting in record profits for many online businesses

SCIENCE & TECHNOLOGY

Some of the most successful businesses today were founded on science and technology. In the 1970s, companies such as Apple and Microsoft released groundbreaking computer hardware and software that earned billions of dollars. More recently, companies such as Google and OpenAI have transformed the way people find information.

MEDIA & ENTERTAINMENT

Many successful companies are in the media and entertainment industry. Some, such as Disney and Netflix, create television shows and movies. Others create video games. Sony, Microsoft, and Nintendo are the most popular makers of gaming consoles. Music and books are other big parts of the media and entertainment industry.

FOOD & DRINK

The food and drink industry is made up of many different kinds of businesses. Some entrepreneurs run food trucks or small restaurants. Others build their businesses into large **franchises**. Some manufacture foods to sell in stores. General Mills and Coca-Cola are among the most recognized food and drink brands in the United States.

FASHION

Fashion is a booming global industry. Top brands such as Nike release popular shoes, clothing, and accessories. Many smaller fashion brands are also successful. Some of today's top fashion entrepreneurs combine high-end designs with Earth-friendly **textiles**.

MORE BUSINESSES, MORE ENTREPRENEURS!

HEALTH & BEAUTY

Health and beauty companies sell products and services that improve health and help people look and feel their best. Some sell technology that helps people track their health. Others sell cosmetics, skincare products, and more.

TRANSPORTATION

In the late 1800s, most people traveled using horses, trains, or ships. Cars and airplanes emerged in the 1900s. New businesses manufactured parts and provided services for these new forms of transportation. Today, the transportation industry includes many well-known companies.

KAMEALE TERRY

Kameale Terry is the cofounder of ChargerHelp! Terry got the idea for her business while working at EV Connect, an electric vehicle charging station provider. She took calls from drivers who experienced problems at charging stations. She started ChargerHelp! in 2020. Her company provides maintenance services for electric vehicle charging stations. By 2024, ChargerHelp! was available in 17 states.

MICHELLE PHAN

Michelle Phan is a beauty vlogger. In 2006, she began posting makeup tutorials on YouTube. Her channel's popularity soared! In 2011, she launched her makeup company Ipsy. Subscribers received monthly deliveries of new makeup products. By 2015, Ipsy was valued at $500 million. Phan left Ipsy in 2017 to launch a new cosmetics company.

DAYMOND JOHN

Daymond John is a hip-hop fashion designer. He founded the clothing line FUBU. John started FUBU in 1992 in his mother's basement. He made hats to sell at concerts. FUBU quickly became a popular fashion brand in the U.S. Soon, it attracted global popularity, generating over $6 billion in sales.

KIRAN MAZUMDAR-SHAW

Kiran Mazumdar-Shaw is a pioneer in **biotechnology**. She helped found Biocon in 1978. The company produced enzymes for the brewing, food, and textile industries. It expanded to clinical research and medicine. Today, Biocon focuses its research on affordable medicines to treat diabetes, cancer, and other diseases.

SCIENCE & TECHNOLOGY ENTREPRENEURS

Steve Jobs was a technology entrepreneur best known for cofounding Apple. Under his leadership, the company released many cutting-edge products. His innovative mindset transformed technology!

Steve Jobs

"Don't let the noise of others' opinions drown out your own inner voice."
—Steve Jobs

EARLY EXPERIENCE

Jobs was raised by his adoptive parents in California. At a young age, Jobs became interested in electronics. As a teenager, Hewlett-Packard (HP) offered him a summer job. There he met Steve Wozniak.

BUILDING APPLE

After high school, Jobs briefly enrolled in college. In 1976, he reconnected with Wozniak, and they founded Apple Computer. They built the first Apple computer in Jobs's parents' garage. Apple I sales reached $774,000 in its first year. Its success led to the Apple II, which was even more successful. Jobs's creative marketing strategies helped build Apple into a successful company. In 1985, Jobs resigned from Apple. He started NeXT, a software and hardware company.

COMPUTER ANIMATION

In 1986, Jobs bought Pixar Animation Studios. Jobs led the company to become one of the most successful animation studios. Its first hit movie was *Toy Story* in 1995. Jobs was Pixar's CEO until Disney acquired the company in 2006.

BACK TO APPLE

In 1997, Apple bought NeXT, and Jobs returned to Apple as CEO. Over the next 14 years, Jobs led the company to develop the iPod and the iPhone. With each new product, he pushed to improve on the previous design. He continued innovating with Apple until his death in 2011.

BORN: February 24, 1955, in San Francisco, California

DIED: October 5, 2011

KNOWN FOR: cofounded Apple and led it to become one of the world's largest technology companies

AWARDS AND HONORS

- **1985** National Medal of Technology and Innovation
- **2012** National Inventors Hall of Fame
- **2022** Presidential Medal of Freedom

SAN FRANCISCO

TIMELINE

- **1968** starts working at HP as a teenager
- **1976** cofounds Apple with Steve Wozniak
- **1986** buys Pixar Animation Studios
- **1997** returns to Apple as CEO
- **2007** introduces the first iPhone

Jensen Huang is CEO and cofounder of technology company NVIDIA. NVIDIA is a leader in **graphics processing units** (GPUs) and **artificial intelligence** (AI).

Jensen Huang

EARLY LIFE

Huang was born in Taiwan in 1963. He moved to the U.S. when he was 9 years old. In 1984, he graduated from Oregon State University with a degree in electrical engineering. He moved to California to work and earned a master's degree from Stanford University.

GAMING GRAPHICS

In 1993, Huang cofounded NVIDIA. NVIDIA started as a **semiconductor** company focused on graphics hardware for gaming. In 1999, NVIDIA released the GeForce 256. It was marketed as the world's first GPU. The GeForce 256 led to a major deal with Microsoft to develop hardware for its Xbox console.

GROWING MARKET

Huang helped grow NVIDIA's market to other technology fields. In 2008, NVIDIA released the Tegra line. This hardware was used in smartphones and cars. It was also used in the Nintendo Switch.

GEFORCE 256

TIMELINE

1972 moves to the U.S.

1984 earns degree in electrical engineering

AI TECHNOLOGY

In 2023, NVIDIA introduced an AI supercomputer. It allows developers to design AI software, analyze data, and program complex **algorithms**. In 2025, NVIDIA announced a personal AI supercomputer called DGX Spark. Under Huang's leadership, NVIDIA continues to innovate.

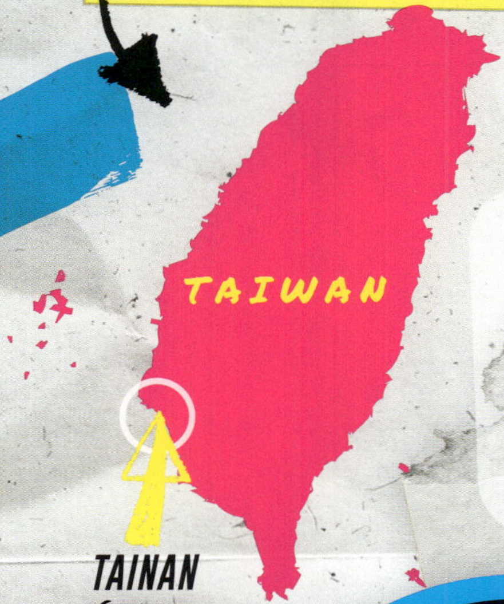

AWARDS AND HONORS

- **2021, 2024** *TIME* 100 Most Influential People
- **2023** *Fortune* World's Best CEO
- **2024** National Academy of Engineering

BORN: February 17, 1963, in Tainan, Taiwan

EDUCATION: Oregon State University, Stanford University

KNOWN FOR: cofounder and CEO of NVIDIA

- **1993** cofounds NVIDIA with Chris Malachowsky and Curtis Priem
- **1999** introduces the GeForce 256 with NVIDIA
- **2023** introduces an AI supercomputer with NVIDIA

Melanie Perkins

Melanie Perkins is cofounder and CEO of the online graphic design tool Canva. The company helps make graphic design easier for people to access.

FIRST SUCCESS

From a young age, Perkins showed an interest in business. When she was 14, she began selling handmade scarves at markets around her hometown of Perth, Australia. While studying at the University of Western Australia, she tutored students in graphic design. This gave her the idea to make an easy-to-use design program. In 2007, she cofounded Fusion Books, an online system for designing school yearbooks.

AWARDS AND HONORS

- **2015** NSW Technology Entrepreneur of the Year
- **2021** Overall Design Collaboration Company of the Year (Canva)
- **2021** Global Business Hall of Fame

TIMELINE

- **2007** cofounds Fusion Books
- **2013** launches Canva
- **2018** leads Canva to reach a $1 billion value after five years
- **2019** leads Canva to acquire Pixabay and Pexels
- **2021** joins the Giving Pledge

ACCESSIBLE DESIGN

Perkins wanted to create a more powerful design tool that could be used for any purpose. She recruited a team to develop the software and found investors to fund her idea. In 2013, she launched Canva. Her online graphic design tool allows users to create professional-quality designs without any technical experience.

ADDING TOOLS

In 2016, Perkins launched a Canva app for iPhone. Canva has also acquired the stock photo websites Pixabay and Pexels. By 2023, Canva had grown to 4,000 employees and 170 million users.

GIVING BACK

Perkins wants to help others. In 2021, she joined the Giving Pledge. Members of this organization promise to donate more than half of their fortunes to charity. As a multibillionaire, Perkins's pledge will make a big impact!

BORN: May 13, 1987

EDUCATION: University of Western Australia

KNOWN FOR: cofounder and CEO of Canva

Jeff Bezos is the founder of the retail company Amazon and the spaceflight company Blue Origin. His work has changed the way people shop, read, and more.

Jeff Bezos

STARTING YOUNG

Bezos started his first business in high school. It was an educational summer camp for young students. After high school, Bezos studied computer science and electrical engineering at Princeton University in New Jersey.

WALL STREET TO WEBSITE

After college, Bezos quickly found success at a New York investment firm. In 1994, he took a bold risk. He quit his job and founded Amazon.com. It opened as an online bookstore in 1995, earning around $510,000 in sales the first year. Amazon soon added more products. By 1999, it was an **e-commerce** leader.

BIG GROWTH

In 2005, Bezos began Amazon Prime, offering free two-day delivery for subscribers. In 2007, he released the Kindle digital book reader. In 2017, Bezos led Amazon to acquire Whole Foods. He also led the company to enter the healthcare market. Today, Amazon is the largest online retailer in the world. It earns over $630 billion each year.

CLIMATE FIGHT

Bezos also founded Bezos Earth Fund in 2020. The organization helps scientists and activists fight climate change and protect nature.

TIMELINE

- **1994** founds Amazon.com
- **2000** founds Blue Origin

BEYOND AMAZON

In 2000, Bezos founded Blue Origin. The company develops technologies to make space travel more accessible. In 2013, he bought *The Washington Post* newspaper. Bezos stepped down as CEO of Amazon in 2021. He continues to work at his other businesses.

ALBUQUERQUE

AWARDS AND HONORS

1999
TIME Person of the Year

2018
National Academy of Engineering

2019
Kenn Ricci Lifetime Aviation Entrepreneur Award

BORN: January 12, 1964, in Albuquerque, New Mexico

EDUCATION: Princeton University

KNOWN FOR: founded Amazon and grew it to become the world's biggest online retailer

2007 leads Amazon to release the first Kindle e-reader

2017 leads Amazon to acquire Whole Foods

2021 steps down as CEO of Amazon

MEDIA & ENTERTAINMENT ENTREPRENEURS

Oprah Winfrey is known for hosting *The Oprah Winfrey Show*. She also founded a television and film production company, cofounded two television networks, and more.

"The big secret in life is that there is no big secret. Whatever your goal, you can get there if you're willing to work."
—Oprah Winfrey

Oprah Winfrey

BORN: January 29, 1954, in Kosciusko, Mississippi

EDUCATION: Tennessee State University

KNOWN FOR: hosted *The Oprah Winfrey Show* and started Harpo Productions

ROUGH START

Winfrey had a tough childhood. When she was 14, she moved to Tennessee. She began doing well in school. She received a full scholarship to Tennessee State University, but she paused her education to pursue her career. She became a news anchor at a local television station.

TALK SHOW HOST

In 1976, Winfrey moved to Maryland. She soon became cohost of a local morning show. Viewers were drawn to her honest and casual personality. In 1984, she moved to Illinois to work on a struggling talk show. The show became *The Oprah Winfrey Show*. Winfrey started a production company, Harpo Productions, and bought the rights to her show. It aired until 2011.

BOOKS AND MORE

Oprah's Book Club was a popular part of Winfrey's show. She shared books she enjoyed, often giving them a huge sales boost. Winfrey published her own content, too. She founded the magazine *O, the Oprah Magazine* in 2000. It was published until 2020.

HER OWN NETWORK

In 1998, Winfrey cofounded Oxygen Media. It is a cable network with programs for women. In 2011, Oprah Winfrey Network (OWN) began. In 2020, Winfrey sold most of her share in the network. But she heads the network as CEO.

AWARDS AND HONORS

- **1994** Television Academy Hall of Fame
- **2000** Spingarn Medal
- **2013** Presidential Medal of Freedom

TIMELINE

- **1985** stars in *The Color Purple* and is nominated for an Academy Award
- **1986** *The Oprah Winfrey Show* goes nationwide, and Harpo Productions is founded
- **1998** cofounds Oxygen Media
- **2000** begins publishing *O, the Oprah Magazine*
- **2011** launches OWN

TIMELINE

1921 starts Laugh-O-Gram

1923 cofounds Walt Disney Studios in California

1928 releases *Steamboat Willie*

1937 releases *Snow White and the Seven Dwarfs*

1955 opens Disneyland

Walt Disney

Walt Disney was a famous animator best known for the many animated movies he created. He used his creativity to build the foundation of what is now a multibillion-dollar business!

YOUNG ARTIST

Disney loved to draw and paint as a child. In high school, he took art and photography classes. In 1921, he started his own company, Laugh-O-Gram. It made animated cartoons. The company soon went bankrupt. Still, Disney did not give up.

DISNEY BEGINNINGS

In 1923, Disney moved to California and started Walt Disney Studios with his brother, Roy. Their first breakthrough came in 1928 when *Steamboat Willie* introduced Mickey Mouse. It was a hit! Other popular characters soon followed, including Donald Duck and Minnie Mouse.

MOVIES AND SHOWS

Disney still wanted to grow the business. He began working on a full-length animated film. *Snow White and the Seven Dwarfs* was released in 1937. It was a huge success! More movies followed, including *Pinocchio*, *Bambi*, and *Dumbo*. Disney produced more than 100 full-length films. He also produced television shows such as *Zorro* and *The Mickey Mouse Club*.

AWARDS AND HONORS

- **1986** Television Academy Hall of Fame
- **22** Academy Awards (individual)
- **3** Golden Globe Awards
- **1** Emmy Award

WALT DISNEY WORLD

THEME PARKS

Disney opened the Disneyland theme park in 1955. It quickly became successful, drawing visitors from around the world. Disney wanted a second park in Florida. But he died before it was finished. Roy carried out the plans, and Walt Disney World opened in 1971.

CHICAGO

BORN: December 5, 1901, in Chicago, Illinois

DIED: December 15, 1966

KNOWN FOR: animator and producer who founded Walt Disney Studios and launched Disneyland and Disney World theme parks

MICKEY MOUSE

"All our dreams can come true if we have the courage to pursue them."
— Walt Disney

Tim Sweeney is the founder and CEO of the video game developer Epic Games. This company is known for developing many popular games, including *Fortnite.*

Tim Sweeney

COMPUTER WHIZ

Sweeney liked building things as a child. Early on, he built go-karts. When he was 11, he tried a computer for the first time. He learned to program and enjoyed playing computer games. After high school, he went to the University of Maryland. In 1991, he started Potomac Computer Systems as a student. The company's first computer game was called *ZZT*.

BIG GROWTH

Early on, Sweeney earned about $100 a day from *ZZT*. He used the earnings to build his business, hiring more employees through the 1990s. Sweeney and his team continued releasing games. In 1999, the company name was changed to Epic Games.

UNREAL ENGINE

In 1998, Sweeney released Unreal Engine. This **game engine** helps others develop video games. It revolutionized the gaming industry. Many modern games use it, including *PUBG: Battlegrounds* and *Yoshi's Crafted World*.

TIMELINE

AROUND 1981
begins programming video games on an Apple II computer

1991
founds Potomac Computer Systems, later renamed Epic Games

HUGE SUCCESS

In 2017, Sweeney's company released its biggest-ever success, a game called *Fortnite Battle Royale*. The game grew very quickly. Within two weeks of its release, it had over 10 million players. Today, it is one of the world's most popular games. Because of it, Epic Games is valued at over $31 billion!

BORN: 1970 in Potomac, Maryland

EDUCATION: University of Maryland

KNOWN FOR: founded Epic Games and created Unreal Engine

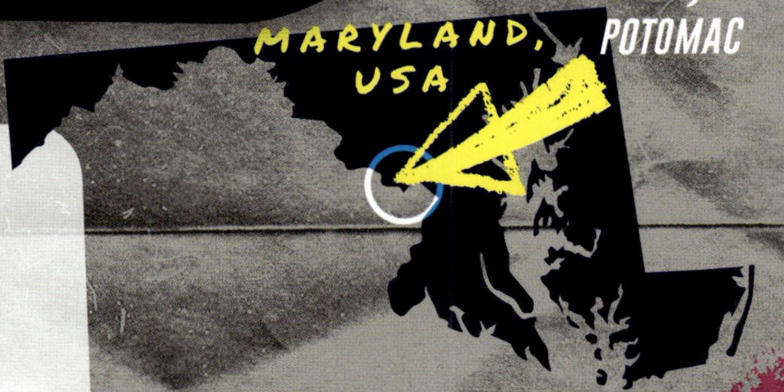

AWARDS AND HONORS

- **2012** Academy of Interactive Arts & Sciences Hall of Fame
- **2017** Game Developers Choice Lifetime Achievement Award

CONSERVATION

Sweeney uses his success to help the earth. He has bought and donated land for conservation. This helps protect the land's plants and animals.

1998 the first version of Unreal Engine is released

2016 donates 7,000 acres of land for conservation

2017 *Fortnite Battle Royale* is released

FOOD & DRINK ENTREPRENEURS

Alina Morse is the founder and CEO of Zolli Candy, a company that makes sugar-free candy. Her candy helps clean teeth while it is chewed.

Alina Morse

CANDY CURE

Morse grew up in Michigan. When she was 7 years old, she went to the bank with her dad. The bank teller offered her a lollipop, but her dad said the candy was bad for her teeth. She decided to make a lollipop that was good for teeth. She launched her candy company at just 9 years old.

THE RIGHT RECIPE

Morse spent two years experimenting and taste testing to find the right recipe. Instead of sugar, Morse used other natural sweeteners. One sweetener, erythritol, is still used today. It fights plaque and reduces bacteria that cause tooth decay. Morse also made the lollipops **vegan** and safe for many types of allergies. She called her candies Zollipops.

SWEET START

With help from her dad, Morse found a factory in Michigan that would make her candy. Her company sold around 70,000 Zollipops in its first year. In 2018, Zollipops sales grew to $6 million.

MORE ZOLLI SMILES!

Morse added other treats to her Zolli Candy line, including Zolli Drops, Zaffi Taffy, and Zolli Caramelz. In 2024, the company released Zolli Gum Popz, a zero-sugar gum pop. Morse's candy is available in over 20,000 stores around the U.S.

AWARDS AND HONORS

2020 Michigan and Northwest Ohio Entrepreneur of the Year finalist

2025 *Inc.* Female Founders 500 list

BORN: May 8, 2005, in Wolverine Lake, Michigan

EDUCATION: Michigan State University

KNOWN FOR: founder and CEO of Zolli Candy

MILLION SMILES

Morse also started the Million Smiles Initiative. It gives Zollipops to schools along with education about keeping teeth clean.

TIMELINE

2012 first gets the idea to create a healthy lollipop

2014 starts selling Zollipops in stores

2018 Zollipops make $6 million in sales

2023 starts studying finance at Michigan State University

2024 Zolli Candy releases Zolli Gum Popz

Mikaila Ulmer

Mikaila Ulmer is the founder of Me & the Bees Lemonade. Ulmer first started selling her lemonade in her front yard as a child. She grew her brand into a multimillion-dollar business.

A SWEET IDEA

At 4 years old, Ulmer was stung by a bee twice in one week. The experience led her to learn more about bees and how to protect them. Around that time, her family encouraged her to make a product for a children's business competition. She made a recipe from an old cookbook. But she made the recipe her own, adding a little honey. She wanted to raise awareness for bees.

CREATING A BUZZ

Ulmer set up a stand outside her home to sell her lemonade. Her company was soon selling lemonade in stores. By 2015, Ulmer's company had made about $40,000 in sales. Ulmer added more lemonade flavors, including mint, ginger, and prickly pear.

AN IMPORTANT BITE

Also in 2015, Ulmer pitched her product to investors on the TV show *Shark Tank*, securing a $60,000 investment. The TV appearance helped boost sales. In 2023, Me & the Bees hit $10.2 million in sales.

TIMELINE

2009 starts selling lemonade outside of her house

2015 secures a $60,000 investment on *Shark Tank*

BORN: September 28, 2004, in Houston, Texas

EDUCATION: Emory University

KNOWN FOR: founder and CEO of Me & the Bees Lemonade

HELPING BEES

Ulmer donates ten percent of the company's profits to groups that support bee **conservation**. She also created the Healthy Hive Foundation to support beekeepers in 2016.

AWARDS AND HONORS

- **2017** *TIME* 30 Most Influential Teens
- **2023** NAACP Entrepreneur of the Year Image Award
- **2023** Afro Tech Future 50

2016 starts the Healthy Hive Foundation

2020 publishes *Bee Fearless: Dream Like a Kid*

2023 Me & the Bees reaches $10.2 million in sales

Ben Cohen is an entrepreneur known for Ben & Jerry's ice cream. He built Ben & Jerry's into one of the most popular ice cream brands.

Ben Cohen

FUTURE PARTNERS

Cohen grew up in New York. He met his future business partner, Jerry Greenfield, in junior high school. As a teenager, Cohen began working at a company that sold ice cream products. After high school, Cohen took creative classes.

MAKING NEW FLAVORS

In 1978, Cohen and Greenfield took an ice-cream-making class at Pennsylvania State University. A few months later, they got a loan to open an ice cream shop in Burlington, Vermont. Their first flavor was vanilla. But Greenfield created new flavors, too. Cohen had a poor sense of taste. Because of this, Greenfield gave his new ice creams unique textures.

IN STORES!

The brand grew quickly. Cohen acted as CEO, and Greenfield was the company president. In 1980, the company began selling pints of ice cream in stores. Ben & Jerry's was worth $30 million by 1987. In 1994, Cohen stepped down as CEO. But the brand continued to grow. Today, it earns millions of dollars annually.

GIVING BACK

Cohen is committed to giving back. In 1985, he and Greenfield created the Ben & Jerry's Foundation. It uses money earned from ice cream sales to give grants. In 2001, the Ben Cohen Charitable Trust began giving money to communities.

AWARDS AND HONORS

- **1988** Small Business Person of the Year
- **1993** James Beard Humanitarian of the Year
- **2023** Anthem Vision Award

BORN: March 18, 1951, in New York City, New York

EDUCATION: Pennsylvania State University

KNOWN FOR: cofounded the Ben & Jerry's ice cream brand

COHEN WITH JERRY GREENFIELD

TIMELINE

- **MAY 1978** starts his first ice cream shop with Jerry Greenfield
- **1980** Ben & Jerry's is sold in stores for the first time
- **1985** starts the Ben & Jerry's Foundation
- **1994** steps down as CEO of Ben & Jerry's
- **2001** starts the Ben Cohen Charitable Trust

FASHION ENTREPRENEURS

Vera Wang is a fashion designer known for her wedding dresses and clothing collections. Her work can be found in many different stores.

Vera Wang

FIGURE SKATING TO FASHION

Wang was raised by Chinese immigrants in New York. Growing up, she was a competitive figure skater. She soon discovered an interest in fashion. After earning a degree in 1971, she began working as an assistant at *Vogue* magazine. She was quickly promoted to fashion editor. In 1987, she left *Vogue* to design accessories.

BRIDAL HOUSE

Wang designed her own wedding dress in 1989. The following year, she opened the Vera Wang Bridal House. At first, she only sold dresses made by other designers. Soon, she began offering her own creations. They quickly became very popular. She expanded her collection to bridesmaids' dresses and evening gowns.

BRAND PARTNERSHIPS

In 2006, Wang partnered with Kohl's department stores to design a more affordable collection of clothing, shoes, and handbags under the Simply Vera brand. She also partnered with many other brands to create jewelry, menswear, and more.

MOVING ON

Wang's brand earns over $700 million each year. In 2024, she sold the brand to a company called WHP Global. However, she continues to work on her brand as its chief creative officer.

AWARDS AND HONORS

- **2003** *Glamour* Woman of the Year
- **2013** Council of Fashion Designers of America Lifetime Achievement Award
- **2021** National Medal of Arts

BORN: June 27, 1949, in New York City, New York

EDUCATION: Sarah Lawrence College

KNOWN FOR: started a line of wedding dresses that led to success in many other areas of fashion

ICE DESIGNS

Wang has designed costumes for numerous U.S. Olympic figure skaters.

TIMELINE

- **1971** starts working at *Vogue*, quickly becoming a fashion editor
- **1990** opens the Vera Wang Bridal House in New York
- **2006** partners with Kohl's to create the Simply Vera collection
- **2019** debuts her 60th bridal collection
- **2024** sells her brand to WHP Global but stays on as chief creative officer

Anifa Mvuemba

Anifa Mvuemba is the leader behind the luxury clothing brand Hanifa. She is known for her revolutionary approach to design and fashion shows. Her clothing has been worn by celebrities such as Beyoncé and Zendaya.

TIMELINE

- **2011** founds Hanifa in Baltimore, Maryland
- **2020** presents the first virtual runway show on Instagram
- **2022** debuts the Live Out Loud collection
- **2023** launches Hanifa bridal collection
- **2024** releases the It Girl collection

A NEW BRAND

Mvuemba's family immigrated to the U.S. from Kenya when she was three years old. In high school, she took a course in fashion design. This inspired Mvuemba to pursue a career in fashion. She enrolled at Morgan State University and learned to sew. She began making clothes for herself and her friends. In 2011, she started the Hanifa brand.

BORN: November 16, 1990, in Nairobi, Kenya

EDUCATION: Morgan State University

KNOWN FOR: founder and CEO of Hanifa who held the first virtual runway show

GOING VIRAL

In 2020, Mvuemba presented her Pink Label Congo collection on Instagram. It was the first-ever virtual runway show. She featured her designs on invisible **3D** models. The show quickly went viral. Two years later, she debuted her Live Out Loud collection on YouTube.

WEDDINGS AND MORE

In 2023, Mvuemba expanded Hanifa into bridalwear. Her collection features a wide variety of fabrics and styles. It includes shoes, veils, and other accessories. In 2024, Mvuemba released a new winter collection that featured textured items and quality knitwear.

INSPIRING OTHERS

Mvuemba's innovative approach to fashion inspires the next generation of designers. In 2020, she started a mentorship program for young designers. She has announced plans to open a manufacturing company to help other designers find the resources they need to succeed.

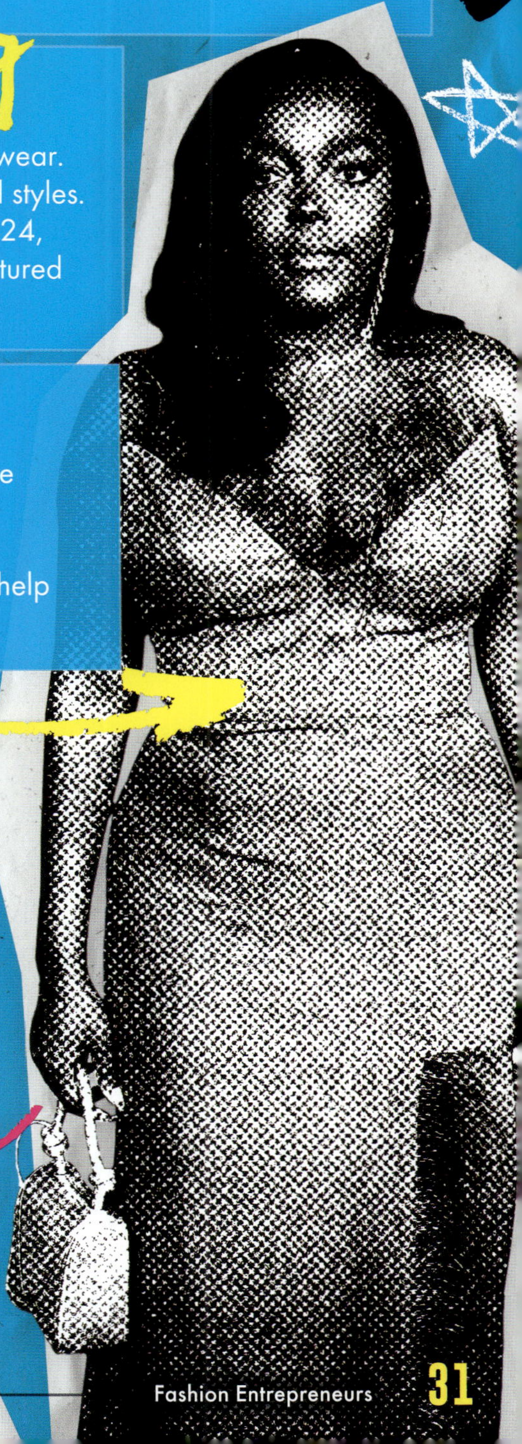

AWARDS AND HONORS

- **2020** — ***New African*** **100 Most Influential Africans**
- **2021** — ***InStyle*** **Future of Fashion Award**
- **2023** — ***Ranks Africa*** **100 Most Impactful People**

Phil Knight is the cofounder and former CEO of Nike, Inc. He grew the company into the largest sport and fashion brand in the world.

Phil Knight

EARLY LIFE

Knight started running track at an early age. While attending college, he joined the track team. His coach was Bill Bowerman, who was known for modifying running shoes for better performance. After graduating in 1959, Knight went on to business school. In 1962, he toured a shoe factory in Japan. He made a deal with the company to sell the Onitsuka Tiger shoe line in the U.S.

NIKE BEGINNINGS

Knight teamed up with Bowerman to form Blue Ribbon Sports. The company sold shoes at track meets. By 1969, Blue Ribbon Sports had sold $1 million worth of shoes. They later split with Onitsuka and renamed their business Nike.

AWARDS AND HONORS

- **2012** Basketball Hall of Fame
- **2020** Champion for Cures Award
- **2024** Stanford University Degree of Uncommon Citizen

TIMELINE

- **1962** travels to Japan to learn more about shoe production
- **1964** cofounds Blue Ribbon Sports, later renaming the company Nike, Inc.

CELEBRITY KICKS

In 1984, Knight signed an **endorsement** deal with NBA **rookie** sensation Michael Jordan. Nike soon launched its Air Jordan line of sneakers. The shoes earned $126 million in their first year. They are still among Nike's most popular shoes.

BIG GROWTH

Knight looked for other ventures, too. In 2003, Knight helped Nike acquire the shoe brand Converse for around $315 million. The following year, he stepped down as CEO of Nike. He remained as chairman until 2016.

SHOE DOG

In 2016, Knight published *Shoe Dog*. It is a book about his personal life and career with Nike.

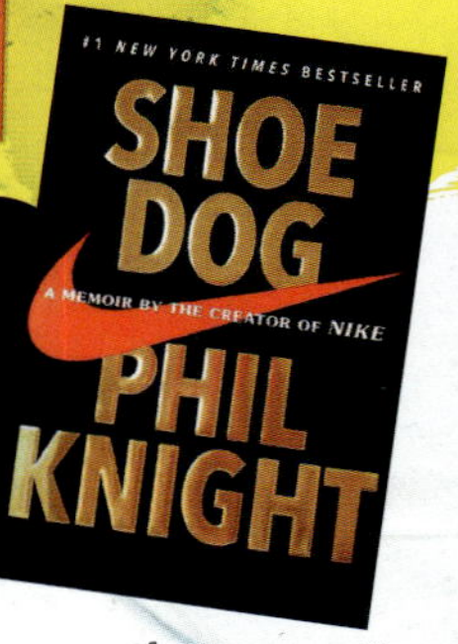

BORN: February 24, 1938, in Portland, Oregon

EDUCATION: University of Oregon, Stanford University

KNOWN FOR: cofounder and former CEO of Nike, Inc.

1984 signs an endorsement deal with Michael Jordan

2004 leads Nike to acquire Converse for around $315 million

2016 retires from role as Nike chairman, 12 years after stepping down as CEO

HEALTH & BEAUTY ENTREPRENEURS

Madam C.J. Walker was an entrepreneur who created a line of hair products for Black women. She was one of the first American women to become a self-made millionaire.

Madam C.J. Walker

A HARD CHILDHOOD

When Walker was born, her parents had recently been released from slavery. She was the first person in her family to be born free. Her parents died when she was young. She had to work at a young age. Eventually, she moved to Missouri. Her brothers were barbers there.

DELTA

BORN: December 23, 1867, in Delta, Louisiana

DIED: May 25, 1919

KNOWN FOR: founded the Madam C.J. Walker brand

FINDING SUCCESS

In her 20s, Walker began losing her hair. She experimented with treatments, creating her own haircare and cosmetic products. In 1905, she went to Colorado for work. She and her husband began advertising her products. Soon, they were manufacturing them in a factory. By 1910, business was booming.

BUILDING THE BUSINESS

The company trained salespeople, called Walker Agents, to be **beauticians**. They traveled throughout Black communities to promote the business and its philosophy. Their goal was not only to sell products. It was also to help Black Americans find more success.

HELPING HER COMMUNITY

In 1916, Walker moved to Harlem, New York. She became involved with the **Harlem Renaissance**, founding and contributing to organizations that improved the lives of Black Americans. She used her wealth to help her community. She continued this work until her death in 1919.

AWARDS AND HONORS

- **1992** Global Business Hall of Fame
- **1993** National Women's Hall of Fame
- **2018** Indiana University Chancellor and Provost Medallion

TIMELINE

- **1887** moves to St. Louis, Missouri
- **1890s** begins experimenting with treatments to prevent hair loss
- **1905** begins advertising her products in Colorado
- **1908** opens a factory and hair school in Pittsburgh, Pennsylvania
- **1916** moves to Harlem and becomes involved with the Harlem Renaissance

Selena Gomez

Selena Gomez is an actress, singer, and the founder of Rare Beauty. Her cosmetic company has grown into a billion-dollar business.

TIMELINE

2007 lands the lead role in Disney's *Wizards of Waverly Place*

2017 teams up with Coach to create the Selena Grace collection

2020 launches Rare Beauty and the Rare Impact Fund

2022 cofounds Wondermind

2024 Rare Beauty is valued at over $2 billion

CHILD STAR

Gomez began acting at a young age. In 2007, she began starring on the Disney Channel show *Wizards of Waverly Place*. Since then, she has starred in many other TV shows and movies. Gomez also pursued a career in music, recording several hit songs.

FOUNDING RARE BEAUTY

Gomez launched Rare Beauty in 2020. She wanted to create makeup that made everyone feel beautiful. Rare Beauty quickly became a top-selling beauty brand. By 2023, it reached $350 million in annual sales. In 2024, the company was valued at over $2 billion.

MAKING A RARE IMPACT

Through Rare Beauty, Gomez works to do good. She gives a portion of every sale to mental health organizations through the Rare Impact Fund. As of 2025, the fund has raised over $16 million.

FASHION FORWARD

In 2017, Gomez partnered with Coach to launch the Selena Grace line of handbags and accessories. They also created a clothing line together.

MENTAL HEALTH HELP

In 2015, Gomez announced she has a disease called lupus. Her symptoms led to a lifesaving kidney transplant in 2017. In 2020, Gomez announced she has bipolar disorder. Her experiences led her to cofound Wondermind in 2022. It is a mental health platform that connects people with community support and tools for managing mental health.

BORN: June 22, 1992, in Grand Prairie, Texas

KNOWN FOR: founded Rare Beauty, released several hit songs, and acted in numerous films and TV shows

GRAND PRAIRIE

AWARDS AND HONORS

- **2020** Beauty Inc Startup of the Year Award (Rare Beauty)
- **2024** Best Social Brand Presence Webby (Rare Beauty)
- **2025** Screen Actors Guild Award

James Park

James Park has a passion for creating great new technology. He is best known as the cofounder of Fitbit. His product has helped people lead healthier lives.

FOUNDING A COMPANY

Park was raised in Ohio. His parents were Korean immigrants and business owners. Their hard work inspired Park at a young age. He left Harvard University to start his own software company. He founded Epesi Technologies in 1999, but the company only lasted about two years.

ANOTHER COMPANY

In 2002, Park cofounded Wind-Up Labs. The company created HeyPix, a digital photo editing and sharing platform. In 2005, CNET bought the company. Park worked at CNET as a director of product development.

AWARDS AND HONORS

- **2015** *Forbes* 40 Under 40
- **2016** Ernst & Young Entrepreneur of the Year

FIT TECHNOLOGY

In 2006, the Nintendo Wii's motion-tracking technology inspired Park. He wanted to bring that technology into everyday life. He and Eric Friedman designed a new style of **pedometer**. They called it the Fitbit.

MANY USERS

By 2021, more than 30 million people around the world used Fitbit devices.

TIMELINE

- **2002** cofounds Wind-Up Labs
- **2005** sells HeyPix to CNET

BORN: 1977 in Cleveland, Ohio

EDUCATION: Harvard University

KNOWN FOR: cofounder of Fitbit

FITBIT STEPS AHEAD

The first Fitbit went on sale in 2009. The company shipped out around 2,000 devices right away and took thousands more orders. New releases brought more features, including stair counting and sleep tracking. Current styles can monitor heart rate and track swimming strokes.

SOLD TO GOOGLE

Over time, Fitbit has sold more than 140 million wristbands and clip-on devices. Park sold Fitbit to Google in 2021 for $2.1 billion. He left the company in 2024.

2009 the first Fitbit device is sold

2021 sells Fitbit to Google for $2.1 billion

2024 leaves Fitbit

TRANSPORTATION ENTREPRENEURS

Henry Ford was an automobile manufacturer who founded the Ford Motor Company. He also developed the assembly line system, which allowed for mass production of automobiles. His company changed everyday life for many Americans.

GIFTED MECHANIC

Ford showed a gift for **mechanics** at a young age. At 16, he took an **apprenticeship** as a machinist for a shipbuilding company. In 1891, he was hired as an engineer for the Edison Illuminating Company.

BORN: June 30, 1863, near Dearborn, Michigan

DIED: April 7, 1947

KNOWN FOR: founder and president of the Ford Motor Company

HORSELESS CARRIAGE

As an engineer, Ford oversaw electric service for Detroit, Michigan. In his spare time, he started working on plans for a horseless carriage. He built the Quadricycle in 1896. It looked like a horse-drawn carriage, but it ran on gasoline.

MAKING CARS AFFORDABLE

In 1903, Ford founded the Ford Motor Company. Its first car was the Model A. The Model T was introduced in 1908. It was the first car affordable for most Americans. In 1913, Ford launched the first moving assembly line. His system reduced production time from 12 hours to around 90 minutes. Eventually, the company could build a Model T every 24 seconds!

A LONG CAREER

In 1919, Ford stepped down as the company president. But he continued to be involved in production. He returned as president from 1943 to 1945. His work changed the world!

AWARDS AND HONORS

- **1928** Franklin Institute Elliott Cresson Gold Medal
- **1938** Institution of Mechanical Engineers James Watt International Medal
- **1999** *Fortune* Businessman of the Century

TIMELINE

- **1896** builds the Quadricycle
- **1903** founds the Ford Motor Company
- **1908** introduces the Model T
- **1913** invents the assembly line system of production
- **1919** steps down as company president, returning for two years in 1943

William E. Boeing

William E. Boeing was an aircraft pioneer who founded the airplane company Boeing. Today, his company is one of the world's largest aerospace companies.

TIMELINE

- **1908** founds Greenwood Timber Company
- **1916** cofounds Pacific Aero Products Company, which later becomes Boeing Airplane Company
- **1927** forms Boeing Air Transport
- **1934** resigns from Boeing after a government ruling forces the company to break apart
- **1940s** returns to Boeing as an advisor during World War II

EARLY LIFE

Boeing grew up going to boarding schools in the U.S. and Switzerland. In 1899, he began attending Yale University. But he soon moved to Washington after inheriting land there. He established the Greenwood Timber Company.

TAKING FLIGHT

Boeing began looking for new ventures. He wanted to learn to fly. He bought his first airplane in 1915. He worked with others to design his own aircraft. In 1916, he finished his first plane, *Bluebill*. He founded Pacific Aero Products Company, which later became the Boeing Airplane Company. The company built aircraft for the U.S. Navy in World War I.

PASSENGER PLANES

Early Boeing planes were not built for passengers. This changed with the Model 80 in 1928. It was designed to carry 18 passengers. This passenger plane led to modern commercial airliners, such as the Boeing 747 and 777.

AWARDS AND HONORS

- **1934** Daniel Guggenheim Medal
- **1966** Aviation Hall of Fame

BOEING MODEL 80A

STEPPING DOWN

In 1927, Boeing Air Transport formed to transport airmail. In 1929, the company merged with several other companies to form United Aircraft and Transport Corporation. Boeing was now a large corporation that both manufactured airplanes and provided air transportation. In 1934, a government ruling split up the company. Afterwards, Boeing resigned but returned briefly as an advisor during World War II.

BORN: October 1, 1881, in Detroit, Michigan

DIED: September 28, 1956

EDUCATION: Yale University

KNOWN FOR: founder of Boeing

THE FUTURE OF ENTREPRENEURSHIP

Technology is rapidly advancing. Consumer demands change quickly. New industries are growing to keep up with the change. Online businesses have become a popular choice for new business owners. It is an exciting time for entrepreneurs!

MORE ENTREPRENEURS TODAY AND BEYOND

STEPH SPEIRS

Steph Speirs is the cofounder and former CEO of Solstice. She founded the company in 2014. It works to provide clean energy to U.S. homes through community-shared solar farms. Speirs left Solstice in 2024. She currently teaches about climate technology and works with several climate organizations.

IQRAM MAGDON-ISMAIL

Iqram Magdon-Ismail cofounded Venmo in 2009. While visiting his cofounder, Andrew Kortina, he discovered that he had forgotten his wallet. This inspired them to create Venmo. Venmo is now one of the most popular ways to send and receive money. The pair sold Venmo in 2012.

RYAN HICKMAN

When Ryan Hickman was 3 years old, he visited a recycling center with his dad. He learned that many cans and bottles end up in the ocean. Wanting to protect ocean animals, he started collecting recyclable materials from people he knew. Four years later, he started Ryan's Recycling Company. The company has recycled over 2 million cans and bottles.

RANA EL KALIOUBY

Rana el Kaliouby founded Affectiva in 2009. The company develops technology that analyzes human emotions through facial expressions and other nonverbal behaviors. In 2021, Affectiva merged with Smart Eye. In 2025, el Kaliouby cofounded a new company that invests in AI-focused startups.

JENK OZ

Jenk Oz was a teenager when he founded iCoolKid, a business that created content for young people. The company was soon renamed Thred Media. It continued to grow, eventually becoming available in 17 languages. Oz also grew the business to offer services to help other businesses reach a young audience. Thred has worked with many popular brands, including Microsoft and Epic Games.

JAHKIL JACKSON

Jahkil Jackson was 8 years old when he started his first business. He lived in Chicago, where many people are unhoused. Jackson wanted to help. He started Project I Am, a nonprofit business that provides supplies to unhoused people. This includes socks, deodorant, toothbrushes, and other essential items. Project I Am has reached 135,000 people in need.

GLOSSARY

3D—three-dimensional; showing length, width, height, and depth.

algorithms—sets of step-by-step instructions that show how to perform a specific task or solve a specific problem

apprenticeship—a program in which a person learns a trade or occupation by training under an expert

artificial intelligence—a computer's ability to do things a human mind can do

bartered—exchanged goods and services for other goods and services without using money

beauticians—people whose job is to style hair and do other beauty treatments

biotechnology—the use of biological processes to produce products, especially medicines

capital—wealth in the form of money or other assets

conservation—the careful protection of something

crowdfunding—funding a business by raising small amounts of money from many different people

e-commerce—related to transactions done on the internet

endorsement—a payment for promoting a product

franchises—businesses in which the owner operates under an already existing brand or business model

game engine—software that includes tools developers use to make video games

graphics processing units—computer devices used to make it easier and faster for computers to show images

Harlem Renaissance—a movement of artistic and cultural expression by Black Americans in Harlem, New York, during the early 1900s

Industrial Revolution—a period during the 1700s and 1800s when the economy shifted from mostly farming to manufacturing with machines

mechanics—the machinery or working parts of something

pedometer—a device that measures the number of steps a person takes

profit—money earned

rookie—a first-year player

seed money—money used for starting a business

semiconductor—a solid material made up of crystals that can conduct electricity

startups—newly formed businesses

textiles—fabrics

tycoons—wealthy, powerful businesspeople

vegan—made without the use of animal products

WRITE ABOUT IT!

- Which entrepreneur do you think is the most successful? **Why?**

- Do you think entrepreneurs should use the money they earn to help others? **Why or why not?**

- What kind of business would you like to start?

ALSO CHECK OUT

INDEX

The images in this book are reproduced through the courtesy of: Featureflash Photo Agency, front cover (Winfrey, Wang), p. 14 (Bezos main); Ben Stanfield/ Wikimedia Commons, front cover (Jobs); PG/ Bauer-Griffin/ Getty Images, pp. 3 (Winfrey), 16 (Winfrey main); Irving Haberman/ IH Images/ Getty Images, pp. 3 (Ford), 40 (Ford main); Jared Siskin/ Patrick McMullan/ Getty Images, p. 3 (Ulmer); Niday Picture Library/ Alamy Stock Photo, pp. 4-5 (main); Johannes Maximilian/ Wikimedia Commons, p. 5 (1800s); Michael Holley/ Wikimedia Commons, p. 5 (1970s); Natee Meepian, p. 5 (2016); Halfpoint, p. 5 (2020); Krakenimages.com, p. 6 (top photo); Hohum/ Wikimedia Commons, p. 6 (bottom photo); Craig Barritt/ Getty Images, pp. 7 (Terry), 38-39 (Park main); Gage Skidmore/ Wikimedia Commons, p. 7 (Phan); The Shark Group/ Wikimedia Commons, p. 7 (John); Hemant Mishra/ Getty Images, p. 7 (Mazumdar Shaw); John G. MABANGLO/ Getty Images, p. 8 (Jobs main); Bernard Gotfryd/ Wikimedia Commons, p. 8 (Jobs bottom); Matthew Yohe/ Wikimedia Commons, p. 9 (Jobs profile); Can Balcioglu, p. 9 (San Francisco); Maurizio Pesce/ Wikimedia Commons, p. 10 (Huang small); Sipa USA/ Alamy Stock Photo, p. 10 (Huang main); Hyins/ Wikimedia Commons, p. 10 (GeForce 256); NVIDIA Corporation/ Nvidia Press Kit, p. 11 (DGX Spark); CarlosTamsui, p. 11 (Tainan); dpa picture alliance/ Alamy Stock Photo, p. 11 (Huang profile); Rhea Nawar/ Wikimedia Commons, p. 12 (Perkins); Jana Schönknecht, p. 12 (Perth); DANIEL CONSTANTE, p. 13 (Canva); Horacio Villalobos/ Getty Images, p. 13 (Perkins main); Brent Lewin/ Getty Images, p. 13 (Perkins profile); James Duncan Davidson/ Wikimedia Commons, p. 14 (Bezos small); Resul Muslu, p. 14 (Amazon box); SeanPavonePhoto, pp. 15 (Albuquerque), 43 (Detroit); Loredana Sangiuliano, p. 15 (Bezos); Van Ha/ Wikimedia Commons, p. 15 (Jeff Bezos profile); CapCase/ Wikimedia Commons, p. 16 (Kosciusko); Lawrence Jackson/ Wikimedia Commons, p. 16 (Winfrey profile); Tibrina Hobson/ Getty Images, p. 17 (Winfrey); lucky-photo, p. 19 (Walt Disney World); Iuliia Sokolovska, p. 19 (Chicago); Boy Scouts of America, p. 19 (Disney profile); Koavf/ Wikimedia Commons, p. 19 (Mickey Mouse); ThatGuyFrom1929/ Wikimedia Commons, p. 19 (Disney main); Epic Games/ Wikimedia Commons, p. 20 (Epic Games); Microsoft Corporation/ Wikimedia Commons, p. 20 (Sweeney main); Official GDC/ Wikimedia Commons, p. 21 (Sweeney top, Sweeney profile); Tony Quinn, p. 21 (Potomac); Diego, p. 21 (Fortnite); Jason Mendez/ Getty Images, pp. 22-23 (Morse); Keith Homan, pp. 22 (Zollipops), 39 (Fitbit); Michael Bezjian/ Getty Images, p. 23 (top photo); Gruban/ Wikimedia Commons, p. 23 (Morse profile); Notorious4life/ Wikimedia Commons, p. 23 (Wolverine Lake); Springwater88/ Wikimedia Commons, p. 24 (Ulmer top); Eugene Gologursky/ Getty Images, p. 24 (Ulmer middle); The Image Party, p. 24 (Bees lemonade); Jim Bennett/ Getty Images, p. 25 (Ulmer profile); Jared Siskin/ Getty Images, p. 25 (Ulmer main); Sean Pavone, p. 25 (Houston); mmaroznaya, p. 26 (Ben & Jerry's sign); Lisa Lake/ Getty Images, pp. 26-27 (Cohen main); Steve Cukrov, p. 27 (ice cream); Scott Gries/ Getty Images, p. 27 (Cohen profile); ADE JOHNSON/ AFP/ Getty Images, p. 27 (Ben and Jerry); mandritoiu, p. 27 (New York City); WENN/ Alamy Stock Photo, p. 28 (dress); Joy Malone/ Getty Images, p. 28 (Wang main); Fairchild Archive/ Getty Images, p. 28 (makeup); The White House/ Wikimedia Commons, p. 29 (Vera Wang profile); Luciano Mortula-LGM, p. 29 (New York City); Dimitrios Kambouris/ Getty Images, pp. 30 (Mvuemba profile), 31 (Mvuemba small); eunikas, p. 30 (Nairobi); Frazer Harrison/ Getty Images, pp. 31 (Mvuemba main), 37 (Gomez main); Ilya S. Savenok/ Getty Images, p. 31 (clothing); Louis Lopez/ Cal Sport Media/ Alamy Stock Photo, p. 32 (Knight small); Gustavo Caballero/ Getty Images, p. 32 (Knight main); Mathieu Landretti/ Wikimedia Commons, p. 33 (Air Jordan shoe); Fma12/ Wikimedia Commons, p. 33 (book); Andy, p. 33 (Portland); Drew Angerer/ Getty Images, p. 33 (Knight profile); Vladimka production, p. 33 (Nike box); Gado/ Getty Images, p. 34 (C.J. Walker main); Wendy Kaveney/ Wikimedia Commons, p. 34 (Hair Grower top); Weatherguy08/ Wikimedia Commons, p. 34 (Delta); Smith Collection/ Gado/ Getty Images, p. 34 (C.J. Walker profile); Heritage Art/ Heritage Images/ Getty Images, p. 35; Mike Coppola/ Getty Images, p. 36 (Gomez); Gabby Jones/ Bloomberg/ Getty Images, p. 36 (makeup); Lunchbox LP/ Wikimedia Commons, p. 37 (Gomez profile); Jacob, pp. 37 (Grand Prairie), 40 (Dearborn); David Paul Morris/ Bloomberg/ Getty Images, p. 38 (Park small, James Park); Kimberly White/ Getty Images, p. 39 (Park profile); Francis, p. 39 (Cleveland); Themadchopper/ Wikimedia Commons, p. 40 (Model T); Oxford Science Archive/ Print Collector/ Getty Images, p. 40 (Ford profile); 6D/ Wikimedia Commons, p. 41 (Ford logo); Spooner & Wells, Inc./ Wikimedia Commons, p. 41 (Ford Quadricycle); PhotoQuest/ Getty Images, p. 42 (Boeing Model 80A); Bettmann/ Getty Images, p. 43 (Boeing small); Carlos Yudica, p. 43 (airplane); Los Angeles Times Photographic Collection/ Wikimedia Commons, p. 43 (Boeing profile, Boeing main); Miljan Živković, p. 44 (generic entrepreneur); Bryan Bedder/ Getty Images, p. 44 (Steph Speirs); Nomi Ellenson/ Getty Images, p. 44 (Magdon-Ismail); Bykalot/ Wikimedia Commons, p. 45 (Hickman); Cairue/ Wikimedia Commons, p. 45 (Kaliouby); Kevin Mazur/ Getty Images, p. 45 (Jackson); David Jensen/ Alamy Stock Photo, p. 45 (Oz).